Bona Drag

Selected Publications by Jeremy Reed

Poetry
Isthmus of Samuel Greenberg (1976)
Bleecker Street (1980)
By The Fisheries (1984)
Nero (1985)
Selected Poems (1987)
Engaging Form (1988)
Nineties (1990)
Red Haired Android (1992)
Kicks (1994)
Pop Stars, with Mick Rock (1995)
Sweet Sister Lyric (1996)
Saint Billie (2000)
Patron Saint of Eyeliner (2000)
Heartbreak Hotel (2002)
Duck and Sally Inside (2006)
Orange Sunshine (2006)
This Is How You Disappear (2007)
West End Survival Kit (2009)

Novels
The Lipstick Boys (1984)
Blue Rock(1987)
Red Eclipse (1989)
Inhabiting Shadows (1990)
Isidore (1991)
When The Whip Comes Down (1992)
Chasing Black Rainbows (1994)
The Pleasure Chateau (1994)
Diamond Nebula (1995)
Red Hot Lipstick (1996)
Sister Midnight (1997)
Dorian (1998)
Boy Caesar (2004)
The Grid (2008)

BONA DRAG

Jeremy Reed

Shearsman Books
Exeter

Published in the United Kingdom in 2009 by
Shearsman Books Ltd
58 Velwell Road
Exeter EX4 4LD

www.shearsman.com

ISBN 978-1-84861-055-2
First Edition

Copyright © Jeremy Reed, 2009.

The right of Jeremy Reed to be identified as the author of this work
has been asserted by him in accordance with the
Copyrights, Designs and Patents Act of 1988.
All rights reserved.

Cover illustration copyright © Luka Young, 2009.
Author photo copyright © Gregory Hesse, 2009.

Contents

Couple	9
Kitchen Notice Board	10
The Final Cut	11
Pills	12
Jaffa Cakes	13
Red Toe Polish	14
Oh No, Not You Again	15
Big City Dilemma	16
Morning Glory	18
Vertigo	20
Pop	21
Campanula	22
Local Universe	24
Marble Arch	25
Oh No, not my Baby	26
Bloody Mary	31

The Future Arrived Too Early

The Future Arrived too Early	34
Floyd's Package Revisited	36
Tipping Points	38
Instructions for Drawing a Map	39
REsearch	40
Endgaming	41
Billy Shakespeare's silver bullet Ferrari	43
Outside the Genome Campus	45
PVC	46

Your Name

Buying Pentel Sign Pens	48
John and Denise	49
Your Name	51
Janine	53
Get Back	55
Peter the Publisher	57
Blue Death	59
Talking of Alan D	61
The Generous Hours	63

Orange Curtain Remixes
I'm in Love with you in 1965	66
I'm in Love with you in 1965 (cashmere remix)	67
I'm in Love with you in 1965 (Eat Your Heart Out Mix)	69
I'm in Love with you in 1965 (Orange High remix)	71
I'm in Love with you in 1965 (Exit Mix)	73

Me Needing You
The Big Purple One	76
A Side: Fuck You Flip Side: Black as Luck	78
Valium	79
Scarlet Begonia	81
Trip Me Up	82
Veggie Goulash	83
You Could Be Lonelier	85
Bound Feet	86
Burroughs portrait by Richard Avedon	88
Me Needing You	90
Selfridges	92
Broadwick Street	94
Camden Encounter	95

Gimme Shelter
Thinking of Trocchi	98
Pirate Sweatband	100
Luscious Lemon	102
No-Go	104
Hanging Round	106
The Age Don't Matter	108
Petunias and Pomegranate Sauce	109
Parrot Tulips	111
Samurai	112
Ends	113
A Difference of Cigarette Angles (Keith and Ronnie)	115
Wakako's Card	117
Sweet Williams	118
Cornflowers	120

What's In a Day	121
Martyn (After Ten Years)	122
Today's Special	123
Posh	125
Coming up Shine	126

For Toyoko

Couple

Two girls, they're mutant Japanese,
cyberpunk hair, purple on black
like a snake headed fritillary:
one has a taupe coloured birth-mark
blotched like a coffee
stain under her right arm:
(the density
hidden under a T-shirt
like a generic tattoo
of the Hiroshima
mushroom):
her friend wears an Anna Lake leopardskin coat—
the label backflipped and showing
its brandname ID:
her hair's cloned like the other's,
as an arty, hybrid flower.
Her scarf streams anemones at the throat
like bright fish satelliting coral:
she's mini-skirted, thin gold ring
caught like a hollow sun in a pierced nostril:
21 or 22
displaced in the lemon West End sunlight,
alien, post-scripted to the end of time.
They're two together, hand in hand
linked like a bracelet
by the thinnest chain.
They're a same sex item, or simulate
love for each other in their cult of two?
I watch them by the Foyles bus stop—
the precinct's a miniature Tokyo—
the girls like punky modified manga cartoons
headed for St Martin's, and me
slowing it all like a real-time photo.

Kitchen Notice Board

A pin spiked through a Posh cutting—
her features like a Japanese cartoon,
I litter green baize with her look
in Hervé Léger, Azzedine Alaïa,
squirted on skinny jeans,
the Karaoke gamine
in red-capped silver heels
giving flash architecture to her walk
sexy as tangoing with a chocolate
exchanged between two tongues: a morning rush
like the vitaminised sunlight,
orange and violet checking in today
like passengers at arrivals,
a day given the earth name Saturday,
my pin-ups, cut-outs, recipes,
punctured with voodoo pins, the cute track marks
holding them down. My oyster recipes,
(I'm vegan), but do food tourism in my head,
are mostly Normandy, the sieved rainbow
refreshed with local calvados
into a fried, deliquescent slither,
a kiss-taste, sea-taste: I make Oolong tea
like cooking China in a bright blue pot,
cut out quantum stuff from New Scientist,
music reviews, a Mac Russian red pout,
a jumbled collage, like peeled wallpaper,
to jab visuals into my need
to feel alive, packaged in the moment,
juiced-up and lively with big city speed.

The Final Cut

A spoon glued to a honey jar,
a glazed gold-brown solid Manuka cone—
the banking stock of myrtle bees;
the beach I'd left atomized in my shoes,
quartz sparkles like molecular earrings:
the past stops anywhere you want it to
in beachy purple weather
1982? 2002?
His T-shirt read Prettiest Boy in The Morgue:
crimson gothic script blocked on pink.
He'd wait on the rubbled jetty,
bony arm angled
on a jutty knee,
his mind copying a tanker's slow crawl
in real time; the horizon's green lacquer
simmery with fins of heat haze.
We met like that, a week of afternoons
that didn't move, and talked music,
same-sex attraction, men on men.
Evenings I'd catch the sun in the kitchen,
anticipating its fire-red free fall
below the horizon, and trade it in my fist
like an orange tennis ball;
and sort out mini-deserts from salty gym shoes,
little mare's tails, stardust in silver trails
leaking their patterns, grainy zigzag tags
I'd sift like galactic pepper,
finger and thumb dusting the gritty pour
from somewhere in the universe
I'd look up to much later in the dark
cooking with star-belts seen from the back door.

Pills

Lee Harwood's *The Man with Blue Eyes*
face up on a trunk for table
Joe Brainard cover (dead
from Aids)—a reminder
I bought this book in 1983
my chemistry
tampered with by benzodiazapines—
the need so coded in my cells
redeeming prescriptions seemed serial:
Boots after Boots, a High Street pharmacy,
lit by a green, like kamikaze suits.
3 doctors and I stockpiled pills
as molecular offensive
thinking their disconnect would do
me to the impossible end.
Today a blue book blue as valium
published by Angel Hair in NY (1967)
scares up bad associations,
tweaks deactivated receptor sites
no longer binding to a habit.
I'm clear, but miss the filter on reality,
the whiteout edits.
September. Blue aqueous skies turn grey
this afternoon, a small press book
for company, and blue again
remembering the pills I kept as scoop
inside my pocket should the lights go out
under the city in the mad rush hour.

Jaffa Cakes

It mattered outside—pink hydrangeas—
a lipstick pink bleeding to mauve and blue
pumped up by iron, like steroids,
and that your black iPod was branded Zen,
a compact Chinese alien
loaded with Turkish pop, and that the day
was Sunday in the rubber universe
and that we sat out back before the rain
banking ideas—I want to be
an image banker, selling corporates
access to colouring facts with imagery,
giving thought-patterns notes, contours,
an individual edge, a quantum leap
out of the grey room into the blue
oxygenated imaginative reality.
And Jaffa cakes, it mattered too
you chose the third and fifth selectively
by looking to negotiate
a symmetry, 38mm
chocolate layered over orange jelly,
54mm diameter,
1gm of flat—I need the specifics
of this McVitie's masterpiece,
a slim-line bite we crunch by scaffolding,
you telling me that the Black Sea's
a deep turquoise—I choose the first and last
as my endgaming do or die
three-layered tangy sponge finality.

Red Toe Polish

The archetypal icon red,
red as a bindi's tilak dot
or a Fujifilm shot
of a close up red traffic light,
garnet, vermilion, scarlet,
ten high gloss oval sex ads on your toes
hissy as hex
shaped like miniature red coffins
twinkling through 10 denier mesh
or aired out loud
in toeless sandals, Russian red,
paprika, Ferrari-red,
samurai red:
and up the stairs down: I'm waiting for you there,
identifiable by your toes,
the red shock upgraded
to lacquered finish, not a chip
like car showroom cellulose,
a fashion moment deputed
by how you walk today,
as though your feet carried a waiter's tray
of ten whisked up bloody marys
supported by your frisky toes.

Oh No, Not You Again

Endemic thinness, it's a line
they share (28–30" waists)
the Rolling Stones in 2005:
a survivor's calorie count,
the liquidation of all fat
like Africa:
bodies like a measuring tape
held vertical
and belted into skinny jeans.
The thin gene subverting biology,
they're 140lbs max
defiant regeneracy:
the singer works out, eats spirulina gnocchi,
runs like he's orbiting the earth
inside his blood, and comes on stage
lean as the written column of a J
anorexic
or like the gap between centimetres
on a plastic ruler
squeezed in the gap.
The two guitarists are facially sagged,
wrinkled like corduroy,
stomachs flat as the surface of Route 66,
and liquid feed on toxins—sambucca,
Wild Turkey, Guinness, vodka +.
The drummer's like an opium paradigm,
a white-haired chinaman sat on a mat,
only he's normal diet, vintage wines.
I pin the Mojo clipping on my board—
a New York press conference at Juilliards,
attend to a full red begonia's
extravagant millinery,
(Oh no, not you again) in June,
the sameness reassuring, like the rain
come on in writing, filling in the yard
like numbers scored in a Sudoku box.

Big City Dilemma

We're mostly running scared. Contact's
spontaneous, or not at all—
I saw you on the Circle Line,
cerise jumper, oriental
30+, in from Tokyo?
lips held like a camellia

gunned open by the winter sun.
Unseasonable, blue January,
you jacketless, the slim ideal
of gay identity, gelled hair
brushed up like black alfalfa seeds,
dead-level, springy in their tray . . .

Our catchlights signalled, twinkled bright,
coding in their telepathy
across the reconfigured crush
of bodies mashed to telescope
into a stretched anatomy,
grabbing for air on Baron's Court . . .

I panicked my way out, the sky
over West London choked by clouds,
the free air, spacious like a Sahara,
and walked my loss into the day,
its pulse beating like a goldfish
rolling a red eye inside polythene,

and bussed my way to the West End,
high on the city's quango mix
of corporate and guerilla clash,
my mind upgrading imagery—
his triangular face, the hurt
trapped in his eyes like a scratched film,

his jumper's raspberry sorbet splash
toning itself in; and jumped out
at Leicester Square, hope against hope
searching the crowds for a pink flash,
letting illusion go, then chasing it
in complex puzzles down the street.

Morning Glory

Impacted purple:
a silent detonation, one then two,
exploding behind heart-shaped leaves,
spontaneous, like we never hear
supernovae ripping the galaxy,
the star imploding at its core

with radioactive energy.
A morning glory builds on light,
spectacularly in our Hampstead patch,
its tug at photosynthesis
placing it like a test pilot
nose up in vertical flight.

Day by day they proliferate:
my one in twenty popped open
like alien intelligence.
I write outside to refocus
their saucer formation, the fuel
sustaining them is solar power

and unpredictably intense
pollution-cleansing thunder showers
shimmery as a jellyfish.
I sit and watch a Boeing's fins
slice through feathery cirrus streaks,
directing words the way I might

attempt through try outs to explain
morning glories to a Martian
perplexed by blinding urban rain.
My successes score on the page
as imagery. The clouds collect
into a giant grey mushroom.

Two neighbouring radios conflict
as noise quotient. I sit back:
a sniff of thunder on the air;
and pour left hand another drink.
Mostly I notice slow tracking
the dominant in purple's pink—

each flower's marked by a cerise undertone.
I've got them now, or so I think
into a sighting. They're full-on;
but still my work's only half done,
my grabbing for a hat and shades
to match my craft against the sun.

Vertigo

Your airbus thrust for Tokyo—
I'm nervous all day, blasts of vertigo
pocketing me inside our flat:
one holed pink sock, one mauve mismatch
alerting me to the contrast
of feet as art objects

confectioned into colour bands.
I'm liquid nerve for your 12 hours
pressurized in the white skyways
operating a DVD armrest
or tracked by alcohol
whooshing inside your head like altitude.

Spring's here with its camellia spill.
At 17 in love with Bert
(his stammer would have peaked on Tokyo)
camellias rained into my eyes:
hearing him try for rho rho rho
rhododendrons, an April fact

come bursting on the garden
the cerise flowers like Campari
stunningly gunned open.
I do my e-mails, click global
for Tulsa or Nagasaki
as though I moused telepathy

across the digital village.
My fear of long-haul keeps me here
shaping a poem in a capital
highjacked by ministerial czars:
warlords with nerves like smoking guns
power-locked into bullet proof cars . . .

Our resident black woodpecker
headcrest like a Red Indian's
dips into spray. You're bound for Narita
full on, while our agile black jewel
stays on my eye a moment flickering
a white feathery tiara.

Pop

It's the soundtrack to our lives
an inherited poppy gene
not helical but Elvis-shaped
iconic DNA,
a new post-1950's strand
responsive each time we hear
a modern flavour in a voice
or edgy uptake of a band
inheriting collective pop
as a modified signature
and washing colours in the mix,
a blue, an urban grey or pink,
and coming on as blood-cleansing
fidgety stimulus, a hook
like an addictive sonic drug
I can't let go all day
deposited in my tune-bank
as banditry, a riff
provoking dopamine
four-bars locked in my neural
circuitry that worry in
and stay
linked to my personality
as what it means to be alive
inside a mood-themed song
brightening big city air
for 2 to 3
colour saturated minutes
of transient wonder
that for the moment's permanent
as anything I'll get
popping info in my cells
as a big and little
sweet-sad flavoured event.

Campanula

A purple epidemic,
it's like the flower held us hostage
in every rootable crack
gunned its real estate take over
front and side and back

a tenacious rip
in bushy undercover on the steps.
Sometimes I hear it active
tugging millimetres in rain,
doing its green thing, chlorophyll

as agent, sense it like a snail
its increase proportionate
to rainy dialogue.
I think between the spaces
for the words I write

build a poem like that
in a room out of the light
the purple flowers indifferent
to my tracks on paper
coming out right?

It's rashed around the house
its green map
like a frothy moat
pouring in gritty fissures,
a hoof-shaped leaf tagging each gap

with an invasive bite.
Sometimes I listen out the rain
throat-high in a steamy bath
hear its likely duration
cushioned by choked weed on the path

and know it's there as fact
its survival linked to mine,
there as a free agent
plotting out its territory
line by knotted line.

Local Universe

Our local universe: blue ozone hole—
Omega refrigerant chemicals
caking damage,
       in my time
and yours 15.19, rainy London
2.10.07, the sky Boeing gray
and thinking of you Toyoko
hairro
in Japanese: I firm the line
I'm writing wishing poetry
was a communicable gene
ubiquitous as cell text:
she tells me Top Shop's racing car green
nail polish hits the season right
like rhyming Ferrari
with hara kiri.
Bacteria in space hitch-hikes to earth
on shuttles, mutating
in micro-gravity:
I read that in my time, and autumn rain
turns analgesic through the afternoon
demanding an upbeat rhyme
that's downbeat too
like dystopia
colliding above line with euphoria,
the two fractionally out of tune.

Marble Arch

Manga-like, Euro-Asian, a red bob,
she swims into the Nikon's viewfinder,
as someone, Akari or Asami?

23? 6 stone, her Selfridges bag
yellow as a duster, or cheese omelette,
her friend depressing the record-button

on her consulting a London Street Guide's
cellular grid; green paisley swirls
mapping out recesses—rain-scented parks—

chestnut trees domed like green golf umbrellas
I track them from a 94,
the window's atomized meniscus of dirt,

so grainily contemporary,
it's the colour of now arrived at speed:
the crowds endlessly reforming

like the 86 million bits of info
programmed into the human brain as patterns.
Shopping's the tempo: Akari?

now trains her Canon on Hime?
red-haired like her, russet curtains
soft as the tip of an unused paint brush,

her London moment's digitised
at 3.45: depleted oxygen
part of species adaptability

at Marble Arch—the two on a corner
under street-frontage: e-mailing back home
the 12 hours difference to an orange Tokyo dawn?

Oh No, not my Baby

July 16. Olga's white
Estonian hair makes breezy tracks
like a palomino
looping its own tail.
I fidget with sound particles

tuning a poem by ear
open tune like a guitar—
the driving riff of 'Brown Sugar' . . .
The strawberry cheesecake that I spoon's
two-tone like a petunia.

Olga's Estonia's as far
as sites I check for metaphor
in my spacy amygdala.
I tell her weirder stuff, a star
in the Aquila galaxy's

haloed by ethyl alcohol
sufficient to pour everyone
a Gordon's or whiskey slammer
for the next five thousand billion years.
The poem's like a quasar

impulsed somewhere in my cells,
its neural blinking regular
as planet KH150.
Olga's at college, part time here
waitressing salami on ciabatta

or a sticky croque monsieur.
Radiohead on the radio,
we talk in snatches, decibels
slamming round, while inwardly
my lines track octosyllables.

I sit outside. A 757
shows fins through blobby violet cloud.
A DTs wino zigzags by.
Olga's bottled in Miss Sixty jeans
windowing something in her head.

My Lapsang Souchong fires the nerves
booting up my hippocampus.
Olga breaks work at three for school,
let's down her platinum hair, its tail
twitchy like summer lightning.

Pop is Dead

You paint me doing conversion
to how I look forensically.
No makeover. I age 10 years
beneath your thumb. The lime green block
in which my left profile floats free

of gravity is a surround
so loud its urban tropical.
I learn to see myself in zero-g
conditions, my detached image
built up by layers to textural

skin tones, the substitute for me
I know in snatches, each fast hit
elusively approximate.
I need a drink to face myself
the way the reconstructed pieces fit.

We're back of the Holloway Road,
your studio sunny as orange peel
the traffic churn edited out.
It's like sitting in a gear box
this close up contact with the real.

You work to Radiohead's palette,
an abstract integrated sound
building its quotient into your style.
I feel emptied as you subtract
whatever bits in me you find

quirkily individual.
My blue beret's a black donut,
my eye rays out intensity
in ways I recognise, full-on
as though its seeing never shuts.

It's cold maintaining this fixed pose,
the music excites being down.
We interact from ten to one,
then free up, you to rework parts
and me to hurry into town.

Bloody Mary

Red icebergs shattered in a glass,
auroral tiara with cracked pepper
Tabasco in the undertow:

it tastes hot, but it's really cold,
like feelings we can't separate
from loving someone, all aspects

slippery as goldfish in a bowl.
A vodka in a scarlet dress
stagy as Ute Lemper,

its temper's unpredictable
like Wasabi and Habanero
or Worcester Sauce tangoing tomato

with a sharp taste of leather.
It's not a gunshot to the throat,
more a slow burn that separates

into component tastes, the lime
gets tweaky if unmollified
by mid-ballast horseradish.

It's a capricious, husky thing,
a ruminative, slow hand trick,
you get to know at gut level,

the vodka underpinning it
raised as raw firepower in the blood,
a CIA agent policing the cells

with a kick like a cobra's hood.
An expat mixed it first at Harry's Bar,
spiked the membrane with a celery stick,

got a red brick crust on the lip,
and knew he'd done it, felt the bite hit in
and raised an eyebrow in silent applause.

The Future Arrived Too Early

The Future Arrived too Early

A beach-house by a green lagoon;
the sea ploughs iambic pentameters
across global effluvia—
condoms, computer discs, an aircraft seat
blown out of a crashed Boeing,
a Kylie love-doll beached and sat

legs open in a striped deck chair,
a porno-clone that's up for grabs,
the detail so good, that she's real . . .
The couple live there in a speeded-up time,
he's a blue sky ufologist
and she a Euro-Thai

abductee
reading a Martian tourist guide
in a black string bikini:
details of a humanoid autopsy
coded into the CD tucked
inside a ferric-orange cover.

He injects the hormone
thyroxine:
(efficacity unproven).
He's back from Area 51,
head full of alien visitations
and rock-storms blown out of the sun . . .

He looks out over junked debris—
an old army amphibious Dodge truck,
a crocodilean landing craft.
The army's inland, locked in Vietnam?
frozen in time, the jungle crystallized
to components of LSD?

He waves to Rudi. She lifts out of time
for 30 seconds and stares on,
her body a holographic insert
in the bleached day. She's very cool,
then reverts back, hair turned breezy,
her shoulders covered by his strawberry shirt.

Floyd's Package Revisited

A cryonics tank in 1984?
I'd left Floyd like a white shark at Alcor,
Big Brothered by a bank of monitors,
vitrified brain
treated with 7.5 molar glyceral,
an astronaut turned alien, finally

assimilated into pop:
the sort who drive a blacked out silver truck
across the city and salute
biological update to mutant:
a Ziggy Stardust with image rehab
for the 21st century?

He's resurrected, cells in tact,
walked all day on a roughed up Norfolk beach,
amnesiac at first, bandaged,
his memory coming back like radio
panning from hemisphere to hemisphere
before he got the signal clear

in stereo?
Blue airman's coat, he'd watched all day for planes,
and tracked a black helicopter's
thermal imaging cameras trained on him,
hunting at low level above the beach,
a chain gun bug, a tank-buster

dissolving into rolling cloud.
Floyd had my poem from 1984
folded behind his new issue plastic,
his pin numbers recoded from the book's
old ISBN. Peeling bandages,
he'd noticed a skin patch was gold

and touch-screened booster alpha waves.
He sat on staggered shingle by a sea
so grey, it could have been the sky
pushing its frontiers at his feet.
The shore smelled pungent like the moon dust reek
he'd got as irritant on a mission;

the particles eating into his suit . . .
He stayed a while, and rewrote my poem,
yellowing from acid decay,
grew confused over his planetary location,
the moon map in his head like re-entry
aimed for a blue turbulent Pacific bay.

Tipping Points

Magnolias collapse like a pink trifle,
a mashed dessert, get flattened underfoot
in cold abrasive thunder showers. I feel
the planet air-pocket in spin
like a plane thrown about by wind
somewhere above the China sea,
the passengers starting to crawl with sweat.
It's a race between tipping points,
a switch to sustainable technology
or collapse: a network blackout,
all power crashed.
One school holiday, lost in blue mirage
hazing the beach, right down on the green tide
a friend grabbed a rubbery octopus
out of it's niche, in a rock corridor,
tentacles grabbing, and its black ink cap
projected over his white shirt,
the stain opening out like a continent,
a sort of blackest Africa.
It's the shock I remember, the black squirt
gunned like a missile launcher, and my friend's
momentary shattering against a rock.
It's my three-button black Jaeger blazer
brings it all back, so too the planet's flip
one side light and the other dark,
but angry, light-polluted and burnt-out,
things getting rocky, as I track
across a pink magnolia littered park.

Instructions for Drawing a Map

Burn a page in Conrad's *Heart of Darkness*:
the scorch-marks of a brown corona
with a blackened frill:
and place the hole over the Milky Way's
dust-choked hazy galactic core;
(a digital image): star clusters raying out
like two fried eggs placed back to back
and photograph your location
inside that roaring gaseous halo
(the space imposed contains 10 million stars).
Cut out the star-belts compact on your map's
tulip-coloured density waves
and fit it to a Smiths' discography—
100 greatest rarities:
and be specific in the choice—
the Japanese 12" 'This Charming Man'
(Tokuma 15RTL3):
Jean Marais in the photograph.
A Cocteau image circa 1953.
Lift out the precise data, that's now shaped
like a blown out tract of the galaxy:
and play the song like mental furniture
re-arranged in the listening:
and transpose all those black holes in your hand
inside this cutting from Record Collector
and torch it, collect the blackened embers,
and disperse them on a lover's body,
and go that way like Conrad did
mapping out futures on the brimming, stinky leaf black river.

REsearch

I'm 2.8 billion
contiguous bits—my genetic code
compacted as a DNA galaxy:
loss in me wide
as the Mississippi, deep
as dark matter in deep space.
Loneliness in me long
as the Pan-American Highway
cracking from Alaska to Chile
like a loopy helix
My thoughts keep repeating and clicking on
Monica's flame-red (false) 2" fingernails
and a heath path I used to cross
reaching to Lene:
my anticipation killing 3 miles
by a quantum leap of mind, my feet
burning with that immediacy.
The October light comes up flat-signed gold
and unrepeatable like cell kill-off
inside my chemistry. It's death I sniff
like a contrail atomised in my blood,
the coolant crystallizing as I feel
the blue shift to a darker deeper mood.

Endgaming

They play Kylie remixes on the floor—
a techno
'Can't get you out of My Head'
The backroom's a black mirrored mortuary.
They do Russian roulette on the state bed—

a one in six chance of a hole
like a car tunnel through the brain,
a glutinous cortical jam.
Endgaming's the new dance. The drug
fires chemical apocalypse

as user chatter.
The cutie with botoxed frown lines
links up with a rocket maker
from Pan Am space travel.
They slow-smooch to 'The Crying Game'—

Billy Mackenzie's operatic take,
slick as Manuka honey, bled
like cherries underfoot.
They talk of cargo, hotel orbiters,
a moon ID card, and the dead

ejected into space to float.
The club's a disused abattoir,
a blank space, silver walls, neutral
as a nuclear bunker.
Boy George stands in a pharaoh's boat

inside the DJ gate.
Rock dinosaurs, sixty something
arrive in mobile biological vans.
They end-state legends. America's dead
from its own smoking gun.

They party under Charing Cross,
the moment loaded as a gun chamber.
The backroom stretchers out its dead
into a Russian hearse. The dawn's
a bloody mary. It's that violent red.

Billy Shakespeare's silver bullet Ferrari

His blond stick-up cowlick's cute butch,
his brogues polished to a chestnut's
pod-cracked wet
mahogany shine, leave bevels
in the expensive Mayfair pile—

his lover's leasehold in Cadogan Square,
Thom Walsingham, a.k.a. patron
to a kept boy loafing his days
in a red and gold kitsch interior—
the bedroom done by Philippe Starck,

his laptop glowing aqua-green
like an aquarium.
He's the poet who never died—
his activity stored in neurocans,
his bite for imagery acute

as a horse scrunching an apple
in a wasp-bullety meadow.
He's Shakespeare, circa 2010
keyboarding sonnets in linear spurts
to unnamed recipients—Kurt Cobain?—

and someone picked up in the street
by Bateman's Buildings after dark,
druggy, indigent, but his match
in champfering a loaded line—
Kit who was bad news in his veins

and got knifed out at Deptford Creek
and swam downriver to escape;
but got banged up in the Maudsley?
He cracks a slab of Valrhona
and tastes Kit in the chocolate's dark

referrals to bitter undertones.
Writing's like doing neurogym:
he needs a drink—a wake up call
to another reality—
Thom back at 6pm, the gift promised

a silver-bullet Ferrari.
He stands beside the open fridge,
mouth open, chilled bottle in hand,
and sees the body parts cut up
and knows it's his familiar friend,

the one Thom killed from rivalry?—
Kit with his streetwise urchin's gift
to be the loser, and the best
who ever wrote, arms and femurs
ready for carving like a Sunday roast?

Outside the Genome Campus

Nasturtiums satellite as outriders,
so orange they're dictionary definition
orange.

Jan's black suede slingbacks riffed with dust
are details in global positioning.
She networks chromosome 22
with Mick in his retro grey flannel Paul Smith suit,
its 33 million bases

gene-rich between messaging
junk.
They weird it outside snapping black chocolate
85% cocoa
for serotonin. Snap.

Snap. Snap.
She diverts to strawberries
her taste buds vowelling a wide O—

blow air on them laced with carbon dioxide
and they triple in glutathione,
their taste still lipsticky, a bright matte red.

PVC

The mould's his Joey fantasy.
The coating on her naughty bits
that squeaks.
He watches Sid and Nancy self-destruct
on DVD. Joe's glued to polymers

designing fallout shelter kitsch.
He likes the long-chain molecules,
their fit.
Sid was too smacked to heft the knife.
He has the story different,

as apocrypha, Sid's white out.
Joe's glitzing up micropore masks
and fuel cells for the shelter.
She stands up with her glitter spray
jeans stuck like a skin makeover.

YOUR NAME

Buying Pentel Sign Pens

The barrel's purple. Japanese:
the colour of a buddleia
and streamlined like a fuselage

a 737 with 3D
coded under the tail.
Kindness turns corners on a mood

that wouldn't give: 3 pens as light
as chopsticks in my hand
extended to Santa's pink lipstick smile,

she bounces happiness inside her eyes
like orange sunshine
rewarding a bowl of oranges,

snug in a turquoise T-shirt and white jeans
at Belsize Stationers,
and knows my Pentel habit—pens that feed

paper like blood my arteries.
Today her left shoulder bra strap
angles a black spaghetti strand

capriciously. Her brother's brain-damaged:
no long term memory.
She speaks of him like we're watching TV

together, close up and he's on.
We share this free space between customers
for brightening. She's brought me food

to sample, parcelled in a sandwich box:
niramish and aloo gobi
with the proviso medium hot.

John and Denise

The city's millions narrowed down to two?
They're my focal point all day
before we meet
5.45pm, nitrogen dioxide 170pbb,
in a dark bar below the street
at Cambridge Circus, the impacted crowds

holding their tension like the silent roar
of a Bacon autopsy, mouth
twisted into oral pathology.
The light I live in films reality
with its resources from extinguished stars.
I take it in, atomized Soho light

new from the street like a bangle
worn weightless on the wrist.
We're under London in our space,
compact around a table, red lampshades
interpreting a resilient mood
that's constant with us, but we sparkle too

defiantly to liberate belief
in obsessions like poetry
and how the individual sustains edge
by staying out there on a wing.
We're obdurate and lyrical and make
a strength of vulnerability,

a closed, adaptive force of three,
oiling the world's shoulder to fit
our angularity.
Benefits keep Denise hungry.
Going it our way you count your own ribs
like sand bars on a beach the sea

has patterned by erosive wear.
We keep our glow and radiate
a warmth to live by, and go back outside
the deeper for the knowing that we've shared,
and concentrate our light into a force
that burns the brighter for our standing there.

Your Name

Leanda Xavian:
sounding like hybrid botany
an iris genus or lily:
you had a dyed red bob
and a moon-shaped face
with the look of an unwritten poem

and lived in Soho's Wardour Street
134
behind an invisible peppermint
painted, oddly anonymous door.
You wrote me letters on hand made papers
tied them with black and red ribbons

like lacing a corset:
the grain of the envelope palpable
as stroking a hardwood table.
You typed my poems in your studio's
10 x 6 astronaut's cabin
dressed in a black kimono

the green dragon on your back
the colour of urban plane trees
resistant to carbon.
Your agoraphobic history
kept you local, 1hr out
and 6hrs in,

like tonic water needed
as a dilutant to gin.
Grief was its core at 12,
your friend drowned herself in a reservoir
and got pulled out like an alligator
haloed with matted auburn hair

puddling oozy mud?
You kept a lemon in your bag
for fragrance, wore stick foundation,
(Shiseido SPF 15):
worked odd days in a gallery
and worm-holed into dark moods like a mole.

Leanda Xavian:
I think of you painting the card
you gave me like a Kabuki,
and of how you pronounced your name
so it rhymed with Genghis Khan
not Soho rain:

and of the quiet you kept, instead of friends,
and your love of mango tea
bought at the Algerian Coffee Store:
and of how your eyes were like wind chimes
responding to a thought, rounding
its edges into tinkling harmony.

You lived confined to a map
of safe streets on your radar:
your aesthetic pure as air,
your black clothes mixed with foggy tops,
your art books and your catalogues
as inner architecture.

We lost each other, like contrails
dissolving over the city;
but sometimes I still bring your name
on to my tongue and keep it there
like a mantra dipped in honey:
an oddly reassuring private game.

JANINE

Your teacher kept Plath stored in neurocans,
cryonic Sylvia's self-destruct
frozen in liquid nitrogen.
He spiked *Ariel* into your veins,
a school-leaver with black boots gloved

like leather tide-marks at the knee.
We'd meet at the Harbour cafe
and hot-wire Plath myth to a sting
of dopamine, your badgy coat
catch-phrasing the Sex Pistols 'Anarchy . . .'

Chain-smoking, rushed by espressos,
your tom-tom beat was empathy
with the hysterical like Plath—
your lateral bipolar shifts of radar
swinging you out across the road,

shredding an essay like origami,
its paper gull's wings in freefall
round your spiky blue-streaked hair.
Your teacher fed you backseat sweets,
kept Plath alive like a tiger

exploding in your chemistry.
He messed your head. Your brain cells shook
like sugar grains in a sachet . . .
you fluffed exams, wrote poetry
like clocking air miles, nerves shredded

like the laddered trapezoid at your knee . . .
You peaked in summer, read so fast
you shoplifted to meet your need,
kept to the beach, sunned in a thong's
miniscule isosceles triangle . . .

Autumn saw you banged up inside.
Fog souped the harbours. Janine mad.
I left weeks later, and recall
our interlude, rereading Plath's
bullet-shaped moods hot-lined to suicide.

GET BACK

I'd be back to
blue gelid winter 1962
lifting a snowball to Sylvia's window:

asking her not to do it (Plath),
finding a signal to arrest
her plugged-in impetus to die,

flighting a poem as a paper plane
with a red nose cone through the letter box,
telling her she can travel back in time

like subatomic particles,
loop up with a happier Sylvia
stirruped on hot chocolate leather,

riding so fast she's atomised
into the future, 2030?
or doing something girlie like counting

black snowflakes stitched on a La Perla
bra?
But Primrose Hill in 1962,

I'd be there, hoping that a stranger's smile,
or kindness coloured by a word
would make the difference in register,

the little shift to hang in there
despite depression blocked for 30 years
like ice cream in the freezer?

Or maybe I'd leave a fur hat,
a Russian balaclava, and push it
enveloped anonymously

into her glacial, off-white hall,
and go of like a penguin through raw snow
hoping she'd wear it with a winning smile.

Peter the Publisher

A sixth sense. Quirky, lateral
instinct for slow-burn cult novels,
leftfielders, 50,000 words

nosed by his testy book radar
for their potential staying power.
Pink cabbage roses on Thai silk,

his shirt's tropicana pattern
is like the office wallpaper's
distinctly boudoir roses at Earls Court.

His logo's loopy earring on a pin
is signature to those who'll luck it out
in fiction rafts, the stacked excess

of Borders tables, slabby pulp
event-horizoned by its hype,
and keep on going, time-released

to make it if they ever do?
He's bored and reads by excerpting,
does jump shots—synopsis and end,

leaves out the middle as filler,
authenticates the real thing as a taste
cactusy as tequila.

Classics? They're spine out on the wall.
Paul and Jane Bowles, Anna Kavan,
Hesse and Pavese, nympho Anaïs Nin . . .

He's Soho. 5 decades bohemian.
Wedges duck pate on his toast,
mixes framboise with Bollinger,

won't surf the slush-pile, feels it on
his pulses if the book is right,
clean as the scent of a board chopped onion . . .

BLUE DEATH *for Jamie McLeod*

Death's like a protein transcription
miscopied in DNA,
fuses blown from the wear and tear
of being present all the time,
feet rubbed out like a retro hot rod's tyres,
despite the Chevy's makeover,

its cool updated bodywork.
Sealed in the capsule of your lift
as a vertical journeyer
12 floors up in Halliday House
I'm panicked by confined pressure
into reviewing endgame signs

flashing on in my head like monitors
in a Heathrow departure lounge.
The city's grained into my skin—
its graffiti loops a subtext
to my cellular hieroglyphs.
I write it into poetry,

my jumpers holed, my beret badged
with subculture agitprop.
Your window out on Islington
grids London into a film-set.
We talk strategy for a book—
Blue Death, as though we've re-branded

cyanosis and cold OD.
Your photos grab urban decay,
use text like a sexual tattoo
on muscle, a vocabulary
of intransigent skin slogans
signalling what it's like for us

caught in the spotlight, being queer.
Our work's the answer. Hit and run,
but leave a mark that's durable,
scar-tissue mapped by creativity.
We sit at cloud level. The light drives in,
blue as a diamond on this sleety day.

Talking of Alan D

The voice so modern it's like orange juice
vitaminizing, optimal,
a sunburst down the entryphone
of city welcome, squeezing Toronto
into Bedford Court Mansions, red brick block
accommodating a Beckstein piano

as central theme, sheet music littering
each surface, his hand-written scores
pencilled in with a green HB:
the impetus abundant as protein,
the librettos obsessive, detailing
how rent turns a trick on a mean punter,

reversing roles so it's the man gets fucked,
humiliated, put in a corner,
the boy calling his gang to do over
the city fat cat; he both writes and draws
his fascination with how loser wins
on terms belonging to the oppressor . . .

He'll make you tea and take notes as you talk,
quizzing a word, a phrase, and keeps a file
on all close friends—a packed sandwich filler
of quirky, confessional biography.
I see mine sometimes, fattening three years,
a blue manilla folder now marked 3

brimming with odd perverse, involuntary
disclosures. Nuts are always provided
and chocolate digestives for the sweet tooth.
Alan's rib-clinging T-shirt's washed out black,
his jeans a second skin, his attitude
in age, that of defiant youth.

Light fills the kitchen like a green opal.
His polythene bags of rent boy photos
document a real time obituary
to dead youth, liquidated by the plague
or drugs, but recreated in his hand
as Soho myths: an Aidan, Wayne or Johnny …

I learn of them through his full commentary,
these fugitives re-photographed for thrills
to meet a fetish, They were on the rack,
pretty sometimes, but eaten by the street.
My friend's their archivist. He sift thousands.
Johnny come Home; but these aren't going back.

The kitchen table fills with body bags
of snappy images, the dispossessed
framed in their moment at Piccadilly.
He has their stories, and if the facts bleach
they share a character, an archetype
he returns to as something he can't reach,

but searches for along Old Compton Street,
a Jamie in the rain? and while we sit
he's missing out on possibilities
to focus on his need. We bunch photos
like people dealing cards, sniffing the pack
at random, but can't make the pieces fit.

It's a history of loss through the decades
he celebrates; the boy who runs away
but never cuts it. Someone's on the badge
he's made and wears pinned right over his heart,
a punky, spotty, street-wise, meanish teen
posed for the camera and looking the part.

The Generous Hours *for John Balance*

You the archival Coil
completist—you saved everything
rudimentary as a badger
stocking its subterranean larder
with collectables, your own

variants of a test pressing,
demos, outtakes, ephemera,
you mapping out a song's chronology
detailed as fish bones on a stripped out spine,
you cared about minutiae

like cells grown in a Petri-dish.
Even dead drunk, you remembered the lot,
a litre of vodka gone down
like an alcoholic lake,
you suddenly a grizzly czar

wintering in an ice palace
switching from vodka to red wine
like finding roses in the snow
30 degrees below zero
delusionally crimson as a glass of Bordeaux . . .

My first time at leafy Chiswick
you have me Coil complete, 4 carriers
brimming with rarities, a stash
so individually personalised
your signature on each was a tattoo

of silver noodled ink.
Your generosity was like a stream
flashing inside you, a clear energy
unstoppable at source.
At Weston super Mare, a river flowed

out of your feet, you said, its force
shattering from a sunken valley.
You were the river's shape inside your chair,
a solid flow searching for fish
like a vigilant gold bear.

You bought a house and turned it into things,
books, music, bibelots and art,
your Crowley collection, your stuff
honeycombed into the cellars,
each stash box like a plastic coffin

never again unloaded in your time,
and now dispersed after your death
like breaking up a life, the parts
scrambled as though a river tore the roots
out of a lightning blasted, sucked up tree.

Orange Curtain Remixes

I'M IN LOVE WITH YOU IN 1965

A skinny face shot by Terry Spencer,
you're 22, I guess, a Mod
in Martian shades
concentrated on the centre-piece rack
of low-rise figure-skimming wool hipsters,
your place, John Stephen's The Man's Shop,
divided by a burnt-orange curtain,
the rain
outside, held in neat suspension,
that's my assessment of the light,
a summer's day, your grey crew-neck jumper
so fitted it's closer to you than skin
and much more obvious. You stand,
one hand supported by a hip,
so cool that you're all attitude,
like 1965 took form in you
as face and chemically-thin line.
The shades provide the ambiguity
I fill in—imagining eyes
the green of peppermint Aero,
focused full on the stitching of a seam,
fabric weight, the precise detail
underlining a jacket vent.
It's Saturday, I sense that in your mood,
a hint of recreation with two friends,
I see time stretch like a cat, Saturday
shopping intensity: the look
the only thing, and yours so sharp it hurts,
and I'm in love with you by freezing time,
doing a quantum-retro, wishing we
were meeting somewhere dodgy in Soho
this side of 2.30 or maybe 3.

I'm in Love with You in 1965
(cashmere remix)

Zero-size
(26" waist): chopstick thin,
hairdo shaped by Vidal Sassoon
pin-up style icon to your friends
(your button-downs are peacock-blue
gingham or black watch tartan)

      Do
   I write a song for you
      blue
  eyes or mint Aero green
  I bought an Aero bar
  to check the shade of green
     I knew
   was inimitably you

        Your grey crew-neck jumper
        so skinny fit it hurts
        in me, a silver cashmere,
        hurts by accenting the ribs
        your place John Stephen's
           The Man's Shop
        remember the orange curtain

     divides
  the shop and how the fitting room
      hides
a skinny face shot by Terence Spencer
  the look the only way to be
  you know about it taking speed
     all night
  and it's (I know) all right

A cloudy orange Saturday
a hint of recreational pull
how many eyes that day
                picked you
as attitude a style guru
it hurts I can't get back to you
to know if you're straight, bi or gay

I'M IN LOVE WITH YOU IN 1965
(EAT YOUR HEART OUT MIX)

        The orange curtain,
        burn-orange, ochre, Jaffa
        you'd have known how orange
        I can only guess
        the tone, an orange drape
        the sort of orange in a shirt
        in 1965 the fit
        on you so skinny that it hurts
        it hurts to think your eyes are blue
        arresting an orange curtain
        dividing the room, orange slash,
        the rain outside detained
        the shades provide the ambiguity
        I fill in with green peppermint Aero
        your look it hurts silver cashmere

on you it hurts
not blue but green
    behind
your shades that mean
they're blackout

              like behind the orange curtain
              a divide that orange
              that Bill Franks calls burnt
              orange the one you saw
              concentrated on the centre-piece rack
              of low-rise figure-skimming wood hipsters

an orange orange
tease the colour
    of orange
ice cream, Bill Franks knew
and you

that moment in the photo
    sizing up
a button-down that's peacock blue

I'm in Love with you in 1965
(Orange High remix)

Your profile
brokers the best look on the street,
and yet I doubt you ever smile
or show attention to the heat
your grey
cashmere so skinny that it hurts
worn to effect that Saturday,

the orange
curtain there as a divide
an orange you might like to change
or even note wanting to hide
a spot
your eye's picked out as a detail,
an orange receding from hot

to neutral,
burnt-orange Bill Franks assures me
just like an orange wall:
your place The Man's Shop, and your grey skinny
cashmere
fitting you so it really hurts
and mapping out in clear

contours
the fact you hardly ever eat
from guilt or burning sweat on floors
sunk beneath Wardour Street:
the rain
so choked up, and your eye detains
the burnt-orange curtain,

orange, not red,
hung as a decorative drape,

>   you quizzing a loose thread.
>   It really hurts your shape
>   your line
>   so cool that it's like an orange
>   I pick up for its shine.

I'M IN LOVE WITH YOU IN 1965 (EXIT MIX)

You and me
the orange curtain
in Bill Franks' memory
burnt orange
or variant tangerine
your ambiguity
and it could rain
maintained behind black shades
and I'm in love with you
in 1965,
in Bill Franks' memory
again
it rains later that Saturday
and you're in Brighton
1965, the sea
mixed blue and Aero green
your blackout eyes
in Bill Franks' memory
burnt orange
or variant tangerine
an aereated
peppermint green
it hurts to see
your grey cashmere
I know your ribs
lack filler skin
that thin
in Bill Franks' memory
the orange curtain
burnt orange
or variant tangerine
ochre or Jaffa
in Bill Franks' memory
Sienna
and behind your shades

the ambiguity
of you
buying a denim button-down
that's peacock blue

ME NEEDING YOU

The Big Purple One

Quality Street
shaped like a purple turtle
the quintessential Hazelnut
toothy nugget
boosting climb-out serotonin

with hooky theobromine
excitables
a Nestle star act
in a Bassey gown
purple as a petunia

electric purple
closer to red-violet
as a sticky artefact
the taste buds spike
for a yummy furore.

Their wrappings a hoopla
in runway confection
a stagy diva
in slippery satin
queening it over

marzipan and nougat
in red and white foils.
They're an addictive puncture
to sugar junkies
an impact-supernova

a gummy caramel
with a sticky whack
that coats like an oil slick.
I go for the big bite
cracking the helmet

but smooth out the wrapper
like working goldleaf
into a pattern
smooth it and pocket it
as a purple reminder.

A Side: Fuck You   Flip Side: Black as Luck

If the look and attitude comes right
you me / me you
+ everything
that makes me blue:
(your jeans give nuder profile than your skin)
and the tomato-red crocosmia's
a part of this, its leggy saffron tips
hissy in the peppery August night—
the you that's in your pulse rate, blood type, noise,
attracting, as you find my lap,
concavely applying pressure to sit
across me—and I bite your lips,
the pink elastic of your cerise string
rising like a tide-line above your hips,
you me / me you
configuring to fuck
to music, and your toe polish
is black as night and black as luck.

Valium

A metabolic smoocher. Blues are 10
feel good milligrams
suppressing rush hour traffic in my nerves.
Yellows are 5 and whites are 2
in a descending scale.
Sometimes I feel I'm squashed down at the ends

like earth, by my own gravity,
the weight of experience at my core
full of dead matter, frozen hurt
like moon rocks pitted on a plain.
Valium has a Roman Emperor's name,
a softener for Diazepam

written on a prescription pad
20 x 5.
Its sweet kill infiltrates fat fast
and is a closer bringing sleep
on nights I cant shut down brain noise
or hit the deep

end of the pool.
It fashions a soft focus mood
round as the tablets, but short term
like an Indian summer's still
intensive glow, before the rain
returns again.

At 17, I had a year
of doing valium for a breakdown
and lived for repeat prescriptions
like poetry.
I'd cash them at a pharmacy
with a menthol green sign and chart

their metabolic curve with tea
at the Sunshine Bakery.
It was their disconnect I liked,
the way I felt removed, set back,
disconnected and unplugged
from continuous reality,

as though living behind dark shades.
Little pharmaceutical comforters
they propped me up until withdrawal
decades later, upended me,
my cells churning for their input
like a car run out of fuel

in the mid-Sahara.
Today I long to re-affiliate
with my consolers, feel the drug come up
like blue wallpaper and screen out
my vulnerability like blinds
slatted on a high window catching sun.

Scarlet Begonia

A scarlet frill cracked open
wavelength range 620—
750 nm:
red pigments come to mind by sound—
Indian red, alizarin,
brazilin, vermilion,
Russian red like Mac lipstick,
and this one doesn't know its name
only the sound I give it
my eye filled with the 83,000 cones
used to decode begonia red
in slow hallucinated September
when everything stands still
like the freeze in a dream movie
with a confrontational killer
wearing a slouched red fedora.
Its stayed a week on red alert
this one ostentatious stripper,
letting a red skirt fall, a bra
in sensual striptease.
My own speed moves at burn-out
impacting in my nerves:
light travels at 700 million mph
and we don't notice it,
but this spilled over red begonia
demands attention right up front
and gets if from me day by day
leaning on the back steps
looking its showy way.

Trip Me Up

A rainy monsoon
green-tinged West End sky,
her traffic-stopping red lipstick
hot from the barrel,
and her name's Laura,
a cool in the vowels
like saying Coca Cola
reminded of its tang
on a hot-cold July day.
We communicate from a barrio
of bricky complexes
getting through by thought
travelling in straight lines,
like slicing an orange.
We get it, we're here for a day,
all age levelled by transience,
consciousness as a light bulb
plugged into the moment's
big or small event,
coming on strong.
There's enough between us
to write a song
or walk to Leicester Square
in unison as two
co-ordinates in the present—
two wonders who have met,
my variants of Laura
phrased like a singer's
pause to separate
meaning in the syllables
by timing it late.

Veggie Goulash

A cowboy dish—goulash deboned of meat—
shallow fried tofu as a substitute,
and while it simmers I nibble your feet,

toes painted green, a Shu Uemura green,
glossed like a vintage racing Jaguar,
and underneath your soles that slightly lean

towards the left, a network of live nerves
communicate erogenous signals:
each gets the fine-tuning that it deserves.

Porcini mushrooms helmeted like buns
merge with paprika surges, tomatoes
hot up their scarlet like tropical suns,

garlic and sautéd onion compound taste,
potato, snout-nosed parsnip and turnip
make lego shapes inside a purée paste,

chunks anthologized for an autumn day,
the texture swarming like an autopsy,
the sage starts to have its linear way.

Your feet do puppets, contract and expand,
their sensual traffic stimulated by
manipulative figures of my hand

that tease from them a sensitivity
that breaks up and reintegrates again
and with renewal more convulsively.

Tempah and cornstarch, somewhere a bay leaf
conspires to tunnel in. I work each foot's
indented fault lines like a diamond thief,

conscious with each mapping of a new groove
connecting as reward, and of the stew's
slow-burn update towards it final move.

You Could Be Lonelier

Listening to Bassey on a Sunday—
'I Will Survive' or 'Goldfinger',
the rehab septuagenarian,
aesthetic like a Burmese cat,
mascara like a black rainbow,
Madame Bassey, Monte Carlo's
gold dust big rocks diva
heals along the ripped frontiers
of my emotional scars
sited in wars
I lost and never won.
Her voice fills up my inner space,
big as her arm-throwing gestures
configurating patterns
of sumptuous loss and tantrums
like tigers in the room.
There's no way of staying on
in life, no extended longevity
beyond the cryogenic freeze
or hanging on until the blip
precipitating black out
accelerates across the brain.
I use my Sunday like pressing a shirt,
getting intimate with it
in small ways, like tasting coffee
for its bitchy itch.
The day's a sunned orange original
in which I have a place
busy at doing nothing special
but listen to her big soundtrack
aching like a voice crawling up the wall.

Bound Feet

Her bound feet mutilated, a size 2
compressed centrepiece of foreplay
16cm from heel to toe

left and right fractionally irregular
are throwbacks to imperial toe sucking—
a pedic diagram to sex.

She's Anna, red bob, 16" corset
dripping black detail like a pansy frill
living like an extraterrestrial

in a room the colour of Battenberg cake
pink and yellow grids framed by jam
in St John's Wood, a mansion block

looking like Prora, a rehab hotel
for Hitler's Third Reich bum-boy coterie.
She models accidentally—

feet isolated as fetish
two mouse-sized pink satin slippers
(toes folded back beneath the soles)

as focal extremities.
Anna for hire's serious money
the naughts bubbly as Perrier—

her anonymity vacuum-sealed.
Her lover works her feet like stocks and shares
to optimal effect: black sun tattoos

inked on pristine magnolia skin,
their sensuality contained in scars
archived like a manuscript,

the poet's nerves coded into the lines,
the way her damage comes up right
the better for its recent fade.

Burroughs portrait by Richard Avedon

The face is anatomically exact,
a stripped, forensic, near exhaustion shot,
seer and seen acutely locked
into a frame,
the St James tie like a silk river run
from a deep collar, pocketed, ice-blue,
fitted, T.M. Lewin, Jermyn Street shirt?
The suit's ash grey: the left hand casually
stops at the navel, like it's a lotus
he's apprehended opening up inside.
Bill looks smoked-out of an outlaw's bunker,
a reptile surfaced to sun on a log
beside a muddy dark green pool.
He's like his books extraterrestrial,
stoned by a deep river melancholy,
the left eye raised above the right,
fractionally, 2cm up,
the eyes occupying separate realities,
the right seeing in gold, the left in pink?
He's a chemical lab, dependencies
written into the genial, down-mooded
resignation of a look cooked
by opiates, circa *Cities of the Red Night*.
He's like an endgame that won't terminate,
a prose-czar bottled in methadone,
a mug shot captive in a whiteout space,
dejected, the lines on his face
so grainy they're testicular.
He works at it, the concentrated style
that's cool, but loaded like a gun.
He stares at his reversed image
in Avedon's lens. He's used up
old world stock, hanging in on time,
a man downloading his genes into text,
his novels and celebrity

insignificant to the post-shoot drink,
the full-on Jack Daniels that's coming next.

Me Needing You

Your text works into me like pop—
impulsive digital alert
from Paris where you fashion shoot
Wakako, in a freezing house,
an unpaid model playing mouse
her shyness like an umbrella
screening the hurt
riffed into her identity.
You're cold, the April wind turning your blood
to cryogenics. I can see
a magnolia blown inside out,
its purple lining ripped apart,
the flowers whipped into violent striptease.
Me needing you
you needing me,
its like the lyric to a song
brimming with blue expectation
and you create the melody
Parisian/Japanese
and me the spiky imagery
that gives words stand-up hair.
I go and buy a Russian army coat,
2 rows of 10 buttons like little suns
and wonder if the wearer turned his gun
to authorized murder.
A cold sun makes a red shark gash
in clouds that pile building blocks North.
Your text update brings you to me,
you're in a gold beret, grey coat,
learning French like scraping black toast
to find language like chunky marmalade
on the shaved surface, speaking broken clips
to a shivery Egyptian,
posed in the Marais, while you shoot
lyricized visuals, and I scratch

a finger-nailed response on my keypad
as though I'm typing text into your skin.

SELFRIDGES

We meet on Duke Street, riffy lemon light
atomized into concentrated haze.
A louche blond, T.M. Lewin Shirt, projects
a stringy Chinese girl on toeless spikes
into an abruptly slammed-up black cab
edgy with traffic-tensions. It's your calm

balances my piled-up vulnerability
at West End danger, a knee or a knife
sprung from compacted crowds? We link fingers
like fastening a bracelet and connect,
squeezing response in little pressure bursts.
The feeling comes up bittersweet like life,

elusive, focused like a rolling storm.
It's boosts of beta-endorphins we need
in Selfridges mansion, film-set interiors
for Toyoko's dress habit, swiping at racks
to scrutinise floating chiffons, black silks,
a squall of red roses bumped on dark blue

slashed by antagonistic green. We search
460,000 square feet of marble,
swishing flimsy designer froth, seasonal
translucencies, like peeling artichokes
to find the right Size 8 for Japanese
skinny: taut satin-skinned torso, flared hips,

and in her instance navigable legs,
high, vertical and routed in black jeans.
We lift from floor to floor, like it's a dream
we float inside, imaginative tourists
in big store orbit, yellow carriers
boxy like sloganed rectangular suns

and exit into mirage, shimmered light,
5pm Oxford Street, grainy high rise
cubed into white sky like a girl's plimsoll
trailing a sneaky lace, and readjust
to what's around, checking into reality,
and feeling her fingers reaffirm trust.

Broadwick Street

He wasn't Jimmy Dean, Billy Fury,
Elvis or Morrissey,
ambivalent quiff proponents;
his smile bright as a Swarovski crystal's
flashy iconography
outside Cowling & Wilcox arts, graphics,
the light that slow, the photons seemed
arrested, like a finger in honey,
his hair sculpted like Jean Marais
into a two-tiered confection,
blond highlights; and the air so still
it seemed like water standing in a bath
before interrogation by a toe.

I could have followed him under the street
where men make assignations in lowlight,
blue wall tiles and CCTV
grainily monitoring each image,
the legend of Johnny Come Home
repeated, re-photographed every day?
I kept myself to myself, busily
preoccupied with my workday menu
(1500 words to complete?)—time out
measured in intervals, optimal sips
at living, went the other way
knowing we'd never meet again, our lives
lost to each other in the city's corridors.

Camden Encounter

Sunday arrives like orange juice
maxed to a vitamin C overhaul.
The way she writes her name the M's
like two people of different height
attempting to support a chair,
the A finds the two levelling a plank
laid on their heads,
the S is a rattlesnake standing up
like a hissy lasso,
an A again, this time a stepladder,
the K's quite literally a kangaroo,
the O's a lemon stood upright.
She's gone again into the crowd,
its pull contagious by numbers
as though somewhere there's a black hole
asserting gravity.
I tilt my purple glasses at the day,
prospectingly; and dive into the mix,
that's tight, chemical as thunder,
gene-pooled with every nationality
and up high with euphoria
as a collective pull.
I disappear like that, led where the stream
dictates, and tell myself
there's an imaginary leader of the pack,
stringing us all along, calling the time
and dressed from head to toe in black.

GIMME SHELTER

THINKING OF TROCCHI

I meet you in the intravenous prose
heroin (diacetylmorphine)
fixed in your veins 5 x a day
a cold dopamine gold rush diffusing
into *Cain's Book*—your scow tied up at Flushing Pier,
the junkie showing ski tracks on his arms
like crushed blueberries and raspberries.
Death's like an email forwarded
to alien intelligence Your copyright's
dissolved like a rainbow, the purple band
the last to vaporize after the pink.
Your contracts dematerialized in print,
Grove Press, John Calder, circa 1962,
your liquidation of rights like a death
you kept on feeding by ripping yourself.
I share your book, or the idea of you
with a friend on this lyrically rainy day
underground at the Beaujolais—
Alex Trocchi whose writing changed the world
into a variant biochemistry,
its fluctuation like the New York tides
pitched to a rhythm like the chasing sea.
You lived with cats in a downgraded flat
and sold rare books on Portobello Road
to supplement a habit. You the legendary
unknown to anyone, blowing on your fingers
outdoors in the cerise cracked, sugar frost.
We speak of you as though you're still alive,
the way a book's a postdated passport
to an intergalactic identity.
Alex's *Cain's Book*, spine out on the shelf,
compactly ageing, acid degenerative,
we keep it with us as contemporaneous
with moving downstream, downtown in our lives,
no re-locatable past, and we talk of that,

to turn back's like muddying ballet shoes
in a wet field, and still the rain holds up
over Soho, the London rain
you must have heard, the junkie bookseller,
generous, bandaged, unable to write
for 30 years, sunk on green methadone
like sea fog rolling slowly through the night.

Pirate Sweatband

Black stretch cotton gloved on my wrist:
the gold skull and crossbones logo
is like a snakeshead feeding on its kill,
a carve-up in embossed glitter
designed by my Japanese friend
and gifted to my writing hand

for its marauding traffic with taboo.
He took it off and gave it me
still drenched in Dolce & Gabanna:
his right and left hands advertising piracy,
his fingernails painted black like the marine sluts
who cruised as terrorists on the high sea

and now track cargo on a computer.
Their legacy's like that other outlaw,
Keith Richards, and his toxic chemistry,
the Stones as a black eye-patched coterie,
a rascal band—they blow you right apart
with riffs that explode like a reactor.

My friend, he's punkish Manga, cartoon hair
and black eyeliner, and gets lost in books,
his identity dissolved like sugar
in what he's reading: Burroughs or Fante.
He wears lenses coloured like crème de menthe
and does immediate updates on his looks.

He's on the street, fired-up by small detail,
or colour-coding a shirt with a cloud,
an eye-shadow with a buddleia,
the two of us, and our vocabulary
so rich with visual pulls, we mix colours
to fit with our shape-shifting reality.

I wear his wristband attacking the page,
a pirate signalling for metaphor,
the gold embossed sun blazing with each shift
of rhythm in my hand, like real sunlight
finding me out in its long journey here
through countless galaxies of burnt-out stars.

Luscious Lemon

My eyes do windows on the street
at St Giles High, mid-afternoon,
the sky a city no-colour
subtexted opium poppy blue—
Dusty Springfield singing 'Sandra'

with posthumous immediacy
at First Out on the cafe stereo
bringing to mind her hairdo's
blond unreconstructed cool,
a platinum diva's beehived cone . . .

My lemon cake's rainy-day moist,
an irregular rectangle
with a daffodil yellow eye.
I sit waiting for Patricia
a decade lost to anonymity

and blue West Coast Pacific fogs,
we of the same small provenance,
our island birthplace tooling genes
peculiar to insularity,
our accent kept as undertow

to re-branded identities . . .
Sunday fills in with tie-dyed clouds
and memories of Patricia Quaid
buying her first fugitive gay paper
in red lipstick matching her heels

on our foggy St James' Street.
I finger Anna Kavan's *Ice*—
the book's osteoporotic spine
telling its age, its poetry
hard as a diamond's rayed-out shine

and sight the street for someone small
inimitably glamorous,
long curtained hair, red lipstick gash?
to cut through crowds and think I see
the exact answer hurrying my way.

No-Go

Fog bunching on Parliament Hill,
blue atomized skeins finning East,
I pivot there, raw December,
the city's block-shaped monitors
lit up all day, its rainmakers

burning out on 300k,
Viagra, coke and Taittinger . . .
A sparrowhawk screams overhead,
its bullety reconnaissance
zooming in on a shattered wood,

querulous as an outrider
zigzagging through canyoned tailbacks . . .
The cold kicks in, I come alive
mapping London's degenerative
Square Mile botoxed in toxic soup

and try to plot my territory,
the safe and no-go interzones
diffused across its villages
like modular cells dividing,
and feel the fog as skin on skin

contact, a sheened intimacy,
broken a moment by a sun
chilly as a bloody mary . . .
I live in this, my only time,
rubbed out by the same energies

as build and reconstruct my genes,
this little space in which I try
to measure bits of poetry
against a star-cooked universe
banged out of the same chemistry,

and hold my fear up on this height,
acutely vulnerable, afraid
of gangs, gay-bashers, yardie rule,
and hear the sparrowhawk hit hard
and direct like the speed of light.

Hanging Round

Take poetry, it needs that space,
my time left uncommissioned by
the corporate, my wrong foot right
in hanging round Piccadilly
trying to tweak your eye

by a telepathic zap,
a scratch
like a migrant eyelash
boating across the cornea.
All of my life I've filled the days

with poetry, its teeming cells
kicking in imagery
nose up to the stratosphere,
my status zero, I won't play
to lick the cherry on

the macaroon.
I write dead level to the street
for beat,
or get drunk on an honest red
to boost neurotoxins.

Hanging round's my prerogative,
I like the drop-hour 3pm,
a low blood pressure siesta,
the workers at their monitors,
the poem doing tai chi stretch

like a lizard changing colour.
Take creative writing workshops
their absolute redundancy.
I'd rather give jet fins to metaphors,
while doing radar on eye candy.

Look for me when I'm on the case,
a pen like a gun at my hip
outside the mega-buzzy Boots,
the afternoon laid on my skin,
the word cut like a diamond on my lip.

The Age Don't Matter

I read Elizabethan in this square
a stanza cut like diamond
a moody John Donne
hexagon
fired up by testosterone
you want the White Stripes to redo
spoken. London 3pm December
yellow jasmine in Soho Square
a half hidden purple hellebore
pushed down like a satin dress
in petals to the hips.
20th Century Fox behind my back
(no chinchilla or chihuahuas
in evidence, no lipstick red
limo) only Yamaha bikes
like swamp alligators
in racks at the kerb.
I turn the page to Marlowe
the big ache in his line
bringing combat to subtlety
a poet's martial art.
The year's full of my dead—
an emptiness like finding Harrods
suddenly blacked out.
I stay with my anthology's
closely plotted emotional chart—
broken hearts, death sentences
the rawness of an open grave
under white river fog
that's art.
I up and go. Two men pick up
punching details into phones.
I head off Tottenham Court Road way
nothing left but a strawberry slash
of loud stormy red sun going down on the day.

Petunias and Pomegranate Sauce

I'm sniffy at their headiness,
petunias after thunder ray-gunned out
as solid purple, London-boxed

at Highgate Nurseries, N6,
brimmy with scent—my nose to nose
enquiry lifts on, isolates

as pin number familiar.
The white demand cool summer tan
as contrast, they are cottony—

a white shirt on the beach at Cannes,
white as Monroe's hair in the sun
bleached supra-Aryan.

The purple colour-code my need—
the letter I in Rimbaud's vowels
is purple, like the power supply

to chassis wiring. Like granadilla.
The number on my call display's
Balance's, and we talk petunias,

this afternoon of furry sun,
he texturing a pomegranate sauce
with molasses in Tottenham . . .

He'll bring me recipes. I try
to think colour for his tart confection,
a wallflower red? aniseed red?

the smell of Turkish poetry?
I soak in light. A UV rub.
Balance's sauce turns critical.

We quit. Highgate's tomato now,
a red slash like a comet stripe
or how I imagine Mars radio.

Parrot Tulips

Bought cold for you at Wild Bunch, frilly glower
constrained like a green crab's pincers,
orange and green, sharp as a cactus thought
generating a bright red cactus flower,
(I give them refuge for six hours
before we meet), press a pinstripe jacket
with a lavender silk lining—
knowing you'll note its rainy day sky emphases
and visit online pharmacy
to buy 60 x 10 mg Temazepam
to help restore jerky black and white sleep
to a less patchy equanimity.
I throw looks at my tight lipped orange hostages
placed so incongruously in a jar
like a customised lollipop
and in between times read a Richard Brautigan—
Willard and his Bowling Trophies
for little hints of quirky stimulus
like adding an extra sugar to tea.
I keep checking the time, as though I'm late
and feel my pulse feed on anxiety.
The tulips stay put like an orange sun
arrested by sea fog, a slow coming
towards a winning radiance. They glow
like me anticipating meeting you
outside ubiquitously global Foyles.
Time registers. I tuck into the crowd
and go to meet you with this bunch in hand,
their burning potential, and find you there,
your sunglasses reflecting big white clouds.

Samurai

Your profile darted at in Samurai,
red bevelled lipstick (795
Shu Uemura?)
my inveterate detailist's acumen
hazarding a guess I'm right?
Colour of a coated patisserie
raspberry?
December, and my free-form lunchtime break
finds me on Neal Street purchasing
a postcard of Elvis Presley,
Tupelo, Mississippi 1956—
iconic hair glossed like a black Lincoln,
right knee
forward, the left scissored back,
right hand extended to a girl's,
left knuckled to the microphone,
the sky behind him incandescent blue
(although its throbbing black and white),
the gesture rock-apocalyptically modern?
I buy the card, and write on it in red,
a red approximate to (795
Shu Uemura),
and take it back impulsively
and give it as a time-displaced token
to the red-lipsticked girl in Samurai.

Ends

In a white samurai bandana
he looks like Yukio
Mishima
driving a raspberry-red Toyota
across a military-zoned Whitehall,
a grey sky like the curve of stonewashed jeans

neutral coloured as moon dust
busy with clouds visiting from Russia?
Up front, a black BMW saloon
is skewed, boot open, driverless,
boxes of lab computer discs
spilled on the road, hand-labelled rectangles

glinting like fall-out over the warren
of subterranean
nuclear bunkers. He pouts,
fitting an Evian bottle to his lips
access blocked by security:
his white shorts skimpy as a bikini . . .

His urgency's testosterone:
the man he'll meet is 30+, that hot
he's like a ubiquitous dildo.
He revs the car like sex, chases
a loop back to Trafalgar Square,
his mind still sighting the scenario

like grainy footage, high density discs
coded with a twisted strip
of dark matter information,
or genes extracted from an alien?
He filters back into the stream
of violent metal, guns to open space

along the Mall under a foggy sun,
drives without hands, his needs that hard
it's like a river in his blood,
optimal hormones, as he points towards
a recessed Mews, cobbles like bubble wrap
and window boxes flowering in the yard?

A Difference of Cigarette Angles (Keith and Ronnie)

Richards and Woods—
dark mess of rucked up, slept-in crow-black hair,
an unkempt, dishevelled architecture,
spiky, Red Indian lacquered mops,
are paradigms of angled fags—
resistant cigarette stylists . . .
With Richards the filter's wedged dead centre
like a fixed point of gravity,
the blue spiralling curl of Marlboro smoke
looping back to the nostrils, leathering
the pigment, like the parched terrain
of the red Nevada desert.
Sometimes on stage the cig cooks left corner,
the angle sluttishly accidental,
the campish, defiant affectation,
part nicotine-need, part image.
Wood's is more basic, pedestrian,
as though his lungs have converted to smoke—
inhalation and renounced oxygen
as fuel for living. Ronnie's bonhommie
sanctifies smoking like a Ferrari needs juice,
as a component of chemistry.
His position's right and left of centre
like the parameters of his playing,
a smoker eating up three packs a day,
utilitarian habit.
Richards is cooler—he projects disdain,
the cigarette as need and image accessory,
the hit sanctifying charred lungs
the colour of a chestnut mare.
60 a day, fired-up on nicotine,
his fretwork's concentrated, and his riffs
spectacularly retro: punched in fag
skewed, like the song off-centre, drooping ash

flickering orange, as legs splayed open,
he plugs the power into 'Jumpin' Jack Flash'.

Wakako's Card

She's drawn a Manga rag doll, bright green hair,
a single blue vertical tear,
a deconstructed, shoulderless T-shirt,
slashed red and white, with safety pins
doing neo-punk, neo-human effects
inside a Modigliani card
as counter-aesthetic. Her writing's purple capitals
(my gift of a Pentel sign pen),
child-like and oval like walnuts
without their grainy cheekbones warped in shell.
Yamagashi's too provincial,
anywhere after London shrinks her dead
into a noodle bowl. She's in transit
to Paris, with her mood-boards and design,
her hair feather-cut with a purple fringe,
her body skinny as a teenage boy.
Modigliani's last portrait of his wife,
Dedie Haydn, sees her head tilted, broken by
the object of her look, her husband's wrecked
syphilitic dissipation.
Her mouth's a red enquiring rose: her eyes
like two brown pools overcrowded by rain.
Waka's subtitled it, 'the brink of tears'.
Dedie looks at a hole burnt in her husband's nerves,
that's death, like a shattered window.
She doesn't eat. Her dark green dress
is hurried, like wind patterning a lake?
Waka can't sleep. She feels the night come on
like sunlight in her eyes. She's wired-up nerve.
I wait for her, her bags stashed in my flat,
her card bedside my bed, the rag doll's frown
quizzical, naive, with the downturned red lips
sucked in, like a full-on performing clown.

Sweet Williams

Little bunchy cluster,
vermilion, maroon and Bordeaux Red
all eyes and shyly
drop dead gorgeous
beret-shaped mid-summer sisters

contend with a friable June
reliant on me for water
as I for a chemical need
a Soho dealer.
It's their transience delivers

optimal beauty
runway contestants dressed by YSL
or Christian Lacroix,
but naturals
with sumptuous tonality

played cool: a beetroot one
meditative as a Rothko
bringing me nose down for a scent
that's like a thundery day
welling in a garden

a deep block of memory
like holidaying in Paris
that hot, the city's empty.
These are New World invaders
brought over from Virginia

to a Tudor Brit without
iris-scans or visas
or plant quarantine,
just syphilis and plague
and sweet williams for nectar.

Mine, have me think of pouring
Beaujolais in a glass
and leaving the body stand.
I crouch to them, as though I'd found
in them a codependency

of need in their indifference
to anything, but immediacy.
I'm free
to fill my loneliness like a jumper
holes and all, the torn network

like fishnet.
I face their perfect completion,
green plastic watering can in hand
and leave them to the torrid day
nurtured a little by my attention.

Cornflowers

Tufty blue
redo,
ultramarine with a grey crown
a blue that's YSL and Yves Klein,
I go to 4 stumped up
when down:
August emergents in a pot
outside—improvised biscuit tin,
Sahara cracks sloshed with water,
a slumped mini-Gobi ecology
roughed over by a dusty sun.
I'm confidential with these four,
I've had
enough I tell them—serious—
of being broken up and sad,
dejected and disconsolate
lost in a poem
like an abandoned car
turned over in a field.
Two rogue poppies—red saucered frills
are quarantined in this warped soil,
two-day shareholders in a lot
guzzled by a snail quango.
We've got no true
blue
communications to share,
only the comfort that I feel
of direct silky contact
with the real
in their wiry resilient
claim on my life in opening out
so blue their blue's more upbeat than the sky.

What's in a Day

Manuka honey's tyre-treads gripping toast,
black China tea's insinuating nose,
and on the back steps cool recess,
first sunlight trafficking Vitamin D
into an old scar-tissue site.
An orange poppy with looped neck
twists a silk mini into space,
while up there, registered as cruisy drone,
a white Boeing's shark fins surface through cloud,
circling as though it's hijacked,
the bloodied pilot ragged in the cabin?
I'm West End bound, this is my interlude,
a concentrated inwards place
in which I'm visited by poetry,
the pressure-point it feeds inside my nerves,
an ordinary fact I do
to know some point in living, a climb-out
into a brighter orange altitude,
a line that follows on another one,
like lacing up a shoe in stops and starts
and always incomplete, like food or sex.
I spend my day talking up books
to punters, a *Naked Lunch*, Grove Press, first,
dissociated, piloting my line
through book-speak, islanded at a red desk,
the lighting like a grainy photograph.
Alcohol's what I hit at 6,
a stratospheric mood-shifter, a bend
in thinking that turns lateral,
and back home later, sit the last light out
like watching a movie turn to slow fade,
not knowing anything, why it goes on
or when or how it all comes to an end?

Martyn (After Ten Years)

Ten years dead. Confidentiality report.
X-files. Disinformation.
Zebra and lion steaks topped with tortillas
they're menu now. Or strawberries
sewn with caviar.
The gourmet in you would have shifted both
into a gastronomical gut vault.
I need you back that bad, it's like ten years
I've looked at empty windows of a block
they've shaken down, Heartbreak Hotel.
You died before combination drugs blocked
accelerating HIV.
We called each other darling like a word
massaged to orgasm. You were a monolith,
a slab of constructive support to me,
and now I've lost a wall, a side of life,
and keep your orange Kenzo shirt
as your last purchase and purple receipt.
Death means gone missing, atomized,
dispersed ID, a rip in personality
like a gash appearing on the right wing
of a space shuttle, foam breaking away
on burn-off: disintegration.
The moment finds me eating falafel,
and doing what you can't do, listening
to latest sounds, or punching text
to say I'm late, delayed again
by London Transport satellite error.
Ten years of missed dinners, clothes, sauna sex,
friendships formed like co-ordinating dress,
and ten for me that register like blanks,
or a foggy abstract shot through with holes
I see into sometimes like a window seat
at take-off, looking out into low clouds.

Today's Special

    They're spiky like bondage,
    antagonistic chestnut pods
    clustering in gold edgy September
    over the cafe's chalked-up board
    in white, green, orange, lavender:
— Pumpkin soup served with rye bread or baguette,
    a benzo-druggy ex-pilot
    telling me of his shattering;
    coke-delusions in the cockpit:
— Spaghetti Bolognese—
    a Boeing fins over
    like a highjacked Kamikaze
    white as a shark's belly
    segueing towards a tower:
— Mediterranean Platter-
    the one on anti-psychotics
    tells me he keeps my Bitter Blue
    on the ward, his drugs cash
    so toxic he's turned fridge-shaped
    from fluid retention:
— English Breakfast with French fries
    the pilot's back at me,
    a day patient now, he protests
    he never flew off the radar
    or bounced the Heathrow corridor
    as a bipolar:
— Croque Monsieur—
    the other thinks the Ganges heals
    and wants to walk on it
    defying gravity:
    he's so skewed he does corners on thoughts
    and presciently feels
    president of hallucinated dreams:
— Soup of the day—
    that's me, vegan ministroni,

the colour of an autumn pond,
eaten listening to dialogue
that loops like spaghetti.

Posh

Designer labels like Kamikaze:
one burn-out supersedes the next—
a glammy Donatella Versace—

her brother shot for infecting rough trade,
a size 6 demoted to 4 then 2,
as though the skin's the only garment made

to fit a Manga caricature.
She's up on Christian Louboutin heels,
cobra, with scarlet soles, a red feature

like a lolloping tongue, swank underside,
her g-strings a T cut from a cherry,
the letter on her skin she tries to hide

beneath Topshop black skinny straight leg jeans.
She's pop, a dystopian refugee,
her audience of imaginary teens

vacuumed in space—feathered combs and hair sticks
spiking a weird skyline in two-tone hair,
each little detail noted for the tricks

it plays with image. She's post-Warhol art,
her disconnect the credibility
in every gesture, and her walk on part

so magnified, she's nothing but a star,
an alien infiltrator, human spike,
her minders tipping her into the car

that's always waiting, like a studio
protecting her from psychos and fall-out
and the new century's red Middle East glow.

Coming up Shine

Torrential, liberating June downpour
at 4am—blackcurrant sorbet sky—
a steamy June skewed
off-centre destabilized duvet,
I'm up and alert listening
(and now the CDs reverted to 0)
to hissy Keith Richards' studio demos,
slow leathery blues, a rolling piano
he plays like he's sitting mid-sea,
mid-ship, with water rising to his knees,
a bottle of Jack Daniels by the throat—
a little interlude in sleeplessness
I use against antagonistic dreams
that keep on looping in my hypothalamus—
the gangster sort, the hot pursuit
chasing me into a dead-end alley,
familiar landmarks have all disappeared,
my bed's a mattress in the rain,
cold metal snouts against my neck.
Outside, and lifting into light,
punchy red roses are smashed by the rain
to a littering impacted debris,
and night stock and blotchy evening primrose
sliced by the violent continuity
of sizzling local weather, rain tearing
the soil away—and I deferring sleep,
sitting up, jittery, afraid
of racing, adrenalised blood,
something inside me, a nerve-terrorist
policing my underworld, trying to blow me up,
while I kitchen myself making green tea,
mass my defences and tighten my fist.

www.ingramcontent.com/pod-product-compliance
Lightning Source LLC
Chambersburg PA
CBHW031154160426
43193CB00008B/362